❀ Psalms

DISCOVER TOGETHER BIBLE STUDY SERIES

Leader's guides are available at www.discovertogetherseries.com

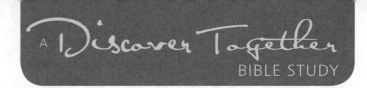
A Discover Together
BIBLE STUDY

Psalms

Discovering Authentic Worship

Sue Edwards

Kregel
Publications

Psalms: Discovering Authentic Worship
© 2012 by Sue Edwards

Published by Kregel Publications, a division of Kregel, Inc., P.O. Box 2607, Grand Rapids, MI 49501.

Previously published by Kregel Publications as *Psalms: Authentic Worship for Today's Women*, © 2009 by Sue Edwards.

All Scripture quotations, unless otherwise indicated, are from the Holy Bible, New International Version®, NIV®. Copyright © 1973, 1978, 1984, 2011 by Biblica, Inc.™ Used by permission of Zondervan. All rights reserved worldwide. www.zondervan.com

Scripture quotations marked KJV are from the King James Version.

ISBN 978-0-8254-4311-4

Printed in the United States of America

12 13 14 15 16 / 5 4 3 2 1

Contents

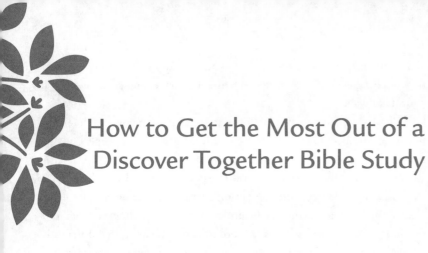

How to Get the Most Out of a Discover Together Bible Study

Women today need Bible study to keep balanced, focused, and Christ-centered in their busy worlds. The tiered questions in *Psalms: Discovering Authentic Worship* allow you to choose a depth of study that fits your lifestyle, which may even vary from week to week, depending on your schedule.

Just completing the basic questions will require about one and a half hours per lesson, and will provide a basic overview of the text. For busy women, this level offers in-depth Bible study with a minimum time commitment.

"Digging Deeper" questions are for those who want to, and make time to, probe the text even more deeply. Answering these questions may require outside resources such as an atlas, Bible dictionary, or concordance; you may be asked to look up parallel passages for additional insight; or you may be encouraged to investigate the passage using an interlinear Greek-English text or *Vine's Expository Dictionary*. This deeper study will challenge you to learn more about the history, culture, and geography related to the Bible, and to grapple with complex theological issues and differing views. Some with teaching gifts and an interest in advanced academics will enjoy exploring the depths of a passage, and might even find themselves creating outlines and charts and writing essays worthy of seminarians!

This inductive Bible study is designed for both individual and group discovery. You will benefit most if you tackle each week's lesson on your own, and then meet with other women to share insights, struggles, and aha moments. Bible study leaders will find free, downloadable leader's guides for each study, along with general tips for leading small groups, at www.discovertogetherseries.com.

Through short video clips, Sue Edwards shares personal insights to enrich your Bible study experience. You can watch these as you work through each lesson on your own, or your Bible study leader may want your whole study group to view them when you meet together. For ease of individual viewing, a QR code, which you can simply scan with your smartphone, is provided in each lesson. Or you can go to www.discovertogetherseries.com

and easily navigate until you find the corresponding video title. Woman-to-woman, these clips are meant to bless, encourage, and challenge you in your daily walk.

Choose a realistic level of Bible study that fits your schedule. You may want to finish the basic questions first, and then "dig deeper" as time permits. Take time to savor the questions, and don't rush through the application. Watch the videos. Read the sidebars for additional insight to enrich the experience. Note the optional passage to memorize and determine if this discipline would be helpful for you. Do not allow yourself to be intimidated by women who have more time or who are gifted differently.

Make your Bible study—whatever level you choose—top priority. Consider spacing your study throughout the week so that you can take time to ponder and meditate on what the Holy Spirit is teaching you. Do not make other appointments during the group Bible study. Ask God to enable you to attend faithfully. Come with an excitement to learn from others and a desire to share yourself and your journey. Give it your best, and God promises to join you on this adventure that can change your life.

Why Study the Psalms?

Today, faithful believers all over the world will open their Bibles to the Psalms—and some will burst into song or prayer. They will sing with others or pray alone. The Psalms speak when we are full of joy but also when unexpected circumstances block the sunshine.

Today in a hospital, at this very hour, someone is whispering into the ear of a dying loved one or a faithful friend,

The LORD is my shepherd; I shall not want. (Psalm 23:1 KJV)

Somewhere a woman is curled up in a large stuffed chair, tears staining her Bible as she reads,

I waited patiently for the LORD;
  he turned to me and heard my cry.
He lifted me out of the slimy pit,
  out of the mud and mire;
he set my feet on a rock
  and gave me a firm place to stand.
He put a new song in my mouth,
  a hymn of praise to our God. (Psalm 40:1–3)

Are they tears of joy or tears of sorrow? They could be either.

Someone experiences forgiveness or sees their newborn for the first time, and the Psalms give wings to their worship as they express their gratitude to God. Someone has just learned they have cancer or that someone they love has preceded them in death. And almost instinctively, as one who is drowning grasps for a lifeline, the Christian reaches for the Psalms.

The Psalms give us permission to express and process our emotions. Psalms is a unique volume in the library of Scripture. In the other books there is more of *God speaking to man*, but in Psalms we mostly have *man speaking to God*. And man is here speaking to God under almost every possible condition and position, and *speaking acceptably*, thus showing us

how *we* may speak acceptably to God under every condition and in every position of life. This is the crux of true and profitable devotional experience (Jensen, *Psalms*, 14).

The Psalms were the songbook of the temple. David, Isaiah, and Jeremiah sang them. Military leaders in the Old Testament celebrated their victories with psalms. At Passover, Jesus sang psalms with his family and later with his disciples. Paul exhorted the Christians at Ephesus and Colossae to "teach and admonish one another with . . . psalms, hymns, and songs from the Spirit" (Colossians 3:16; see also Ephesians 5:19). When we pray or sing the Psalms, we sense the oneness of the church.

And the Psalms will be the songbook of heaven. One day we will gather with the saints of the ages and sing psalms together as we praise our majestic God. What a glorious day that will be! What an incentive to study them, sing them, pray them, and love them.

 Introduction to Studying the Psalms (*11:54 minutes*).

BACKGROUND INFORMATION

In the middle of your Bible is a songbook. The Psalms are lyrical poetry, full of imagery and figurative language. No other book has as many authors as the Psalms. David wrote about half of the 150 songs. Other authors include Moses, Solomon, and some of the song leaders in the temple.

They can be grouped into categories: songs of praise, lament, faith building, thanksgiving, and wisdom. Some are royal psalms because they celebrate earthly kings as well as the King of the Universe. Others are called imprecatory psalms. Their message is "Go get 'em, God," pronouncing curses on one's enemies—not very "Christian." But God wants us to process even these kinds of emotions before we act inappropriately. Consider creating your own system to categorize each psalm so that you can access them later according to your need.

OVERVIEW OF THE STUDY

The purpose of this study is to deepen your worship of Almighty God. What is worship? The term encompasses many aspects of the Christian life—singing, praying, and serving. In essence, worship is responding to God because he alone is worthy. When we worship, we celebrate God's character, works, and plans. We rejoice in our intimate relationship with him. We participate in declaring his majesty and splendor.

The 150 psalms are penned by different authors: Moses (1), Heman (1), Ethan (1), Solomon (2), Hezekiah (10), Sons of Korah (11), Asaph (12), orphan psalms (39), and David (73), although David probably wrote some of the orphan psalms.

Worship can be private or within a community. Some of us raise our hands, sway, and bellow with gusto. Others of us close our eyes, sit in contemplation, sing softly, or kneel. God recognizes and enjoys a variety of worship forms. However, true worship requires that our heart is engaged and our senses are focused on God.

Roadblocks to worship distance our hearts from God. What are typical roadblocks to worship? Discouragement, fear, ignorance, a refusal to deal with sin, distractions, and harboring an unforgiving spirit. Women who worship God freely are hopeful and secure in their identity. They are not plagued by fear. They live productively each day, refusing to allow cares and trials to dissuade them from praising God. They understand redemption and the glorious future that awaits them. Each lesson in our study will tackle one of these roadblocks to help us overcome hindrances to authentic, unbridled worship.

In these busy days, it would be greatly to the spiritual profit of Christians if they were more familiar with the Book of Psalms, in which they would find a complete armory for life's battles, and a perfect supply for life's needs. Here we have both delight and usefulness, consolation and instruction. For every condition there is a psalm, suitable and elevating. The Book supplies the babe in grace with penitent cries, and the perfected saint with triumphant songs. Its breadth of experience stretches from the jaws of hell to the gate of heaven.
—Charles Spurgeon
(*Psalms*, vol. 2, 16)

Celebrate Worship

Connections, Preparation, and Psalm 29

The purposes for this first lesson are threefold: to connect as a community of faith, to prepare together, and to explore Psalm 29, an exemplary song of praise. Assuming that you're doing this Bible study in concert with other women, it's important that you know one another before you take this journey together through the Psalms. If you are already acquainted with everyone, answer the questions that will deepen your relationships. As you prepare to meet with your group for lesson one, you may want to jot down a few notes in answer to the three "Make Connections" questions below. Pray and ask the Lord to give you the courage to be honest and vulnerable with one other. The result should be a richer experience for everyone.

OPTIONAL

Memorize Psalm 29:2

Ascribe to the LORD the glory due his name; worship the LORD in the splendor of his holiness.

MAKE CONNECTIONS

1. Introduce yourself. Talk about your background, family, hobbies, or affiliations.

2. Share about your spiritual background. Are you a Christian, or are you here to investigate the claims of Christianity? Who or what has influenced you on your spiritual journey?

3. What is unique about you? Share something no one else in the group would guess about you.

4. Why are you interested in studying the Psalms? Look over the introductory section, "Why Study the Psalms?" Are you new to the Psalms or are they an old friend? Have the Psalms been meaningful in your life? If so, how?

Out of 219 quotations from the Old Testament in the New Testament, 116 of them—more than half—are from Psalms.

5. As you read the section titled "Background Information," did you learn anything new or interesting about the Psalms?

6. In the "Overview of the Study" section, the term *worship* was defined. Comment on the definition. Do you agree? Can you make any additions that would help the group understand the concept of worship more clearly?

The psalms are the prayers and songs of generations of Israelites who strove to define their relationship to and communicate with the God they called the Lord. The psalms encapsulate the joys, the grief, the questions, and the praises of our ancestors in the faith.
—Nancy DeClaisse-Walford (*Introduction*, 3)

7. Comment on statements related to the different forms of worship. What is your worship tradition? How are you most comfortable worshipping God?

8. Are you respectful of different ways others may worship God? Do some traditions make you uncomfortable? Discuss.

9. Several roadblocks to worship are listed. Have any of these been road-blocks for you? Do you continue to struggle with any of these issues? If so, which ones? Share if you are comfortable.

10. What do you hope to gain in your study of the Psalms? What are you anticipating as you gather with this group? Share any expectations or apprehensions.

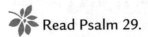 **Read Psalm 29.**

CALL TO WORSHIP

11. As we worship the Lord, what should we be thinking about? Why is he, and he alone, worthy of our worship? (29:1–2)

GOD'S GLORY IN THE STORMS

This middle section of the psalm (29:3–9) paints three pictures of places where God rules.

12. What is the first picture (29:3)? Describe the scene. What does God's voice sound like?

13. Have you ever been in a thunderstorm at sea? Have you seen a film depicting the power of raging waters? What can you add to the discussion to bring this picture to life?

I love to sit on my patio during a thunderstorm. The sound of booming thunder, the lightning flooding the sky, the torrents of rain that nourish the earth—it all speaks of the power, might, and majesty of Almighty God. I love to worship in the rain.   —Sue

 Stormy Seas (*3:31 minutes*). Have you come face-to-face with God's omnipotence? Evidence of God's mighty power should evoke our awe, wonder, respect, . . . and gratitude.

14. What do you think is the author's main point in verses 4 and 7?

15. We find the second picture in verses 5–7, where the psalmist talks about two mountain ranges. They are Mt. Lebanon and Mt. Hermon (also known as *Sirion*). These mighty mountains to the north of Canaan rise to an altitude of ten thousand feet above sea level. Cedar trees on Mt. Lebanon were known for their enormous size. With these facts in mind, what do you learn about God's power from verse 5?

The psalmist describes the earth as responsive to the Creator. Mountains, valleys, fields, and stars are said to shout for joy and sing in the presence of God. The earth is also responsive to humanity expressing a mutual recognition that the earth and humanity need each other. The earth mirrors our own rhythms and suffering. In this interdependent relationship between the earth and humanity, nature suffers or flourishes by our hand. Sharing in our brokenness, the earth is in travail, waiting for the redemption of the children of God, according to scripture. As co-creature, the earth waits with hope for wholeness and restoration.
—Lilian Calles Barger
(*Chasing Sophia*, 110)

16. What does God do to the mountains in verse 6? How does this illustrate his glory and power?

17. The author has painted a picture of God's power over the sea and the land. Where else does God reign? What does his voice cause there (29:8)?

18. What do you think the psalmist is saying with these three pictures?

19. Describe God's actions in 29:9. What is the response of the people? Why do you think the people in the temple respond this way? What would be your response to this sight?

GOD'S SOVEREIGN CARE OF HIS OWN

20. The author concludes the psalm with another picture that is related to a past event. What is the event (29:10) and what two things did God do there (see 2 Peter 2:5)?

21. What does the Almighty do for his beloved, even in the midst of the storms of life (29:11)? Have you experienced these blessings in your own life? If so, please share.

22. Why should we worship God with our whole heart and focus?

Worship is a rediscovery of liturgy, an enhancement of community, an atmosphere of celebration, a new appreciation of environment, new ideas in participation, declaring God's worth, admiring God's character and delighting in His works; worship is God's plan for us; worship is a matter of art and of the heart.
—Ron Allen and Gordon Borror (*Worship*, 7)

Celebrate Intimacy

Psalm 139

Who are you? Does God really know and care about you or are you just a speck in an impersonal universe, a product of time and chance? Your answer will define your life and relationship with your Creator. Psalm 139 provides direction for anyone struggling to understand their identity in Christ and their value to God. Knowing who you are and who God is will also impact the quality of your worship.

Before you begin . . . a question for personal reflection:

Think about how you perceive yourself. Do you see yourself as valuable and precious with a voice and purpose? If so, praise God. If not, consider why not. Who or what has influenced you otherwise? How do you think God wants you to think about yourself?

OPTIONAL

Memorize Romans 8:38–39

For I am convinced that neither death nor life, neither angels nor demons, neither the present nor the future, nor any powers, neither height nor depth, nor anything else in all creation, will be able to separate us from the love of God that is in Christ Jesus our Lord.

 **Read Psalm 139:1–6.**

DOES GOD REALLY KNOW YOU?

Verse 2 contains a merism, a device of rhetoric in which a listing of parts represents the whole.

1. According to Psalm 139:1–4, how well does God know you? What is he aware of all the time?

2. Are you surprised that the Creator and Sustainer of the entire universe takes the time to search for you and know you? If so, how does that change how you feel about yourself and God?

3. Can you know God as well as he knows you? What do the following
   verses reveal?

   Psalm 139:1–6

   Isaiah 55:8–9

   Romans 11:33–34

4. God reveals certain truths so that we may know him better. What do
   these Scriptures teach us about our relationship with God?

   John 10:14

John 14:6–9

1 Corinthians 13:12

My running and my resting are alike within thine observation. I may leave thy path, but thou never leaves mine. I may sleep and forget thee, but thou dost never slumber, nor fall into oblivion concerning thy creature. . . . Behind us there is God recording our sins, or in grace blotting out remembrance of them . . . our Heavenly Father has folded His arms around us, and caressed us with his hand.
—Charles Spurgeon
(*Psalms*, vol. 2, 326-27)

5. Explain Psalm 139:5 in your own words. (See also Psalm 34:7.) Are these words comforting to you? Do you think they are comforting to everyone? Why or why not?

6. In verse 6, David expresses his wonder at this divine knowledge. What words would you use to verbalize similar thoughts?

DIGGING DEEPER

God's omniscience is evident in verses 1–6. Define this attribute of God. What do these verses tell us about God's abilities?

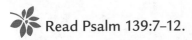 Read Psalm 139:7–12.

IS GOD REALLY NEAR TO YOU?

7. The psalmist asks two questions in verse 7. What are they and what is the answer?

DIGGING DEEPER

The last part of verse 8 actually reads, "If I make my bed in *Sheol*, you are there." What can you discover about the place described by the Hebrew word *Sheol*?

8. According to the author, what are some of the places where God is present? How do you feel as you read about God's proximity?

9. What do the following verses teach us concerning God's constant presence and concern in our lives? If you had doubts about his nearness and care before, how might these Scriptures convince you otherwise?

Jeremiah 23:23–24

Matthew 28:20b

Romans 8:38–39

10. Protection and guidance are evident in Psalm 139:10. The same promise with almost identical words is found in Isaiah 41:10. Why do you think God uses the illustration of his hand holding us?

11. Have you ever said something similar to the psalmist's words in 139:11? If so, when? Did God light up the darkness for you? Can you share a time when you especially felt the presence or protection of God?

DIGGING DEEPER

God's omnipresence is evident in verses 7–12. Define this theological concept, and explain what these verses tell us in relationship to this idea.

 **Read Psalm 139:13–18.**

CAREFULLY AND PURPOSEFULLY MADE

These parts of my frame are all thy works; and though they be close under my own eye, yet are they wonderful to the last degree. They are within my own self, yet beyond my understanding. We need not go to the ends of the earth for marvels; they are abound in our own bodies.
—Charles Spurgeon (*Psalms*, vol. 2, 329)

12. God says that he saw you and knew you before anyone else did. He planned and created you to look the way you look, with your personality and aptitudes (139:13, 15–16). What is your reaction to this truth?

13. What is the psalmist's response (139:14)? Can you wholeheartedly echo these words? If God knew and loved you before you were born, do you think you should place a high value on yourself? Do you? Why or why not? Discuss.

Self-Love (*3:14 minutes*). Do you struggle with loving and accepting yourself? Sue can relate.

14. How is God's sovereign control over life revealed in verse 16? (See also Job 14:5 and 42:2.)

DIGGING DEEPER

Read Proverbs 3:1–2. How might keeping God's commands *prolong* your life? Do Psalm 139:16b and Proverbs 3:1–2 contradict each other? In what sense can both be true?

15. What are the social and political ramifications of Psalm 139:13–16? Discuss respectfully.

DIGGING DEEPER

God's omnipotence is evident in Psalm 139:13–18. Define this theological term and wring out the text to discover how it supports this attribute of God.

 **Read Psalm 139:17–24.**

THE PSALMIST'S RESPONSE TO GOD

To worship is to quicken the conscience by the holiness of God, to feed the mind with the truth of God, to purge the imagination by the beauty of God, to open the heart to the love of God, to devote the will to the purpose of God.
—William Temple, Archbishop of Canterbury

16. Why is the psalmist praising and thanking God in 139:17–18?

17. Respond to the truths in this lesson: God knows you, he is near to you always, and he has designed you perfectly for his purposes. Express your praise in words, music, or art. If you are comfortable doing so, share your creation with your group.

18. The success of our enemies can make us feel frustrated—even unloved by God. David expresses the same sentiments in verses 19–22. What does David ask God to do?

19. See Psalm 139:10, 1 Corinthians 10:13, and Philippians 4:13. What does God ultimately promise to do about the evil and trouble that exist in the lives of believers?

20. The author concludes the psalm with a request. What five verbs are used in these last two verses? In your opinion, what is the psalmist asking God to do in his life? Would you be willing to give God permission to do the same in your life?

21. Does it really matter how you feel about yourself? Is valuing yourself a narcissistic concept that teaches you to be self-absorbed, or a healthy prerequisite for spiritual maturity? Discuss.

22. In light of new insight you've gained from this psalm, how will you think or act differently?

23. How might valuing yourself influence the way you worship your Creator?

Celebrate Hope

Psalm 42

It's one of those days! The nurse's voice on the other end of the line delivers a bad test result. That unexpected expense puts you in the red. The funny engine rattle turns into a loud whirr, leaving you stranded and missing an important meeting. Sometimes "one of those days" turns into one of those weeks—or years. Maybe the person you once adored gets on your nerves more and more, and you wonder where the relationship is headed. Another change looms and you've only just adjusted to the last one. When you try to pray, you feel like you are trying to talk to someone who left town without a forwarding address. You can't seem to muster the energy to face the day. And you certainly don't feel like celebrating. Even devout Christians experience these emotional lows now and then. David did too.

In Psalm 42, David describes times when he was so discouraged that he wanted to give up—but he didn't. Woven into the verses are David's antidotes to discouragement. Study and sing Psalm 42 for a lift out of the blues and into the sunshine, where you can celebrate hope.

 **Read Psalm 42.**

David is believed to have penned this psalm. The "Sons of Korah" were probably men who led worship in the temple (Walvoord and Zuck, *Bible Knowledge*, 825). Note that Psalm 42 is introduced as a *maskil*. Thirteen of the psalms carry this label. How are they different from other psalms? The term probably comes from the Hebrew word *sahkaal*, a verb that means "to be prudent, circumspect, wise—to have insight." Maskil psalms are written to help us gain wisdom and insight when we are dealing with particular situations (Swindoll, *Living Beyond*, 105–6). Psalm 42 is designed to instruct us when we are spiritually dry and discouraged.

Hope is a wonderful gift from God, a source of strength and courage in the face of life's harshest trials. . . . Put simply, when life hurts and dreams fade, nothing helps like hope.
—Charles Swindoll
(*Hope Again*, 1)

Debarred from public wor-
ship, David was heartsick.
Ease he did not seek, honor
he did not covet, but the
enjoyment of communion
with God was an urgent
and absolute necessity,
like water to a stag.
—Charles Spurgeon
(*Psalms*, vol. 1, 173)

1. What word picture does the author paint in 42:1? Envision the scene.

In this psalm, we gain a
glimpse into *the dark night of
the soul,* an experience that
may send even the most
devout believer into a time
of discouragement and
sadness. But look at the
psalmist's ultimate expression
of turning back to God with
hope. We study the psalms
to prepare for our own *dark
night of the soul,* should God
allow that in our future, as
preparation that will lead
us out of the darkness into
his wonderful light. —Sue

2. Have you ever been terribly thirsty? Have you desperately needed
   something that you could not obtain? If so, how did you feel? What
   did you do? Please share.

3. What does the psalmist long for, but seems unable to find (42:2)? Have you ever felt the same way?

A FOUNTAIN OF TEARS

4. What is the psalmist's emotional condition (42:3a)? How do you think his physical health is affected?

In the darkness of our emotional wrestling with God, we grow in our understanding of Him. When He does not respond to us as we expect, we learn about His surprising character. We attack Him with anger, but we do not receive judgment in return. We plead desperately for Him to save us from terror, but He does not necessarily rescue us with immediate resolution of our circumstances. However, what He does reveal is His heart for us.
—Dan Allender and Tremper Longman (*Cry of the Soul*, 39)

5. Can you recall a time when you felt this way? If so, why? Share with the group if you are comfortable.

 Dark Night of the Soul (*4:06 minutes*). Have you battled depression, a *dark night of the soul*? Sue shares her personal story of God's help in recovery.

COMFORTING FRIENDS

Did you ever take a *real* trip down inside the broken heart of a friend? To feel the sob of the soul—the raw, red crucible of emotional agony? To have this become almost as much yours as that of your soul-crushed neighbor? Then, to sit down with him—and silently weep? This is the beginning of compassion.
—Rev. Jess Moody (Cory, *Quotable Quotations*, 76)

6. How are people around the psalmist reacting (42:3, 10)?

7. How did one of Job's friends react to the great tragedies in his life (Job 4:7–8)? Has this ever happened to you? If so, when?

8. What did Job say in response (Job 6:14–21)? What are the lessons for us?

DIGGING DEEPER

Paul praised his brothers and sisters in the Corinthian church for the comfort they provided when he was struggling and discouraged. Read 2 Corinthians 1:3–11. How did the Corinthian Christians minister to Paul? What lessons can people-helpers glean from these verses to help them be effective as they minister to the disheartened?

9. Comforting the discouraged is an art. Can you share any dos or don'ts? (No names, please.) Any related insight?

EMOTIONAL ISSUES

In my best moments, when I calm down and listen closely, God says, "I didn't ask you to become new and improved today. That wasn't the goal. You were broken down and strange yesterday, and you still are today, and the only one freaked out about it is you."
—Shauna Niequist
(*Cold Tangerines*, 39–40)

10. The psalmist writes that he "pours out" his soul to God (42:4). Job's friends reprimanded him for emotional outbursts (Job 15:12–13). When are these outpourings healthy? When are they destructive? Is it wrong to pour out your honest feelings to God? Why or why not?

11. God is an emotional being and he created us with emotions, so we know that emotions can be good. Nevertheless, at times, they can hinder our spiritual growth and make us difficult to live with. What have you learned about healthy and unhealthy emotions that might benefit the group?

CELEBRATING TOGETHER

12. What did the psalmist do previously that he is now unable to do (42:4)?

Think of standing before the tabernacle in the days of David or in the Temple in later years. Imagine worshiping with believers of a bygone era. Put yourself in the ensemble or in the chorus as it lifted its praise to God who lived then, who is alive today, and who will live forevermore. In other words, enter into the sweet spirit of praise, join the anthem of exaltation, and let the hymnbook of ancient Israel become part of your spontaneous worship of God your Savior.
—Robert Alden (*Psalms*, 6)

13. Can you think of any possible reasons why he might no longer be able to participate? Would this limitation grieve you? If so, why?

14. How might the remembrance of these celebrations help him now that he is discouraged?

15. What past hallmarks of God's faithfulness can you recall in your own life? How might thinking about these times help you when you are feeling downhearted?

DIGGING DEEPER

Study David's Psalm of Thanks in 1 Chronicles 16:7–36. Why was David grateful? How did he express his gratitude in the verses that follow the psalm (verses 37–43)? How might a thankful heart lift a sad spirit?

MOOD ENHANCERS

16. Now the psalmist talks to himself (42:5). What does he say? Where does he find solace? Name some ways you have learned to "pick up your spirits" when you are down.

17. What is another way the author tries to gain perspective (42:6)? Has this ever been helpful to you?

"God's holy mountain" was Mt. Zion or Jerusalem.

18. The author is speaking from Mt. Mizar, which is a peak in the Mt. Hermon range (42:6b). Where does he long to be instead (see Psalm 43:3–4)?

19. Have you ever been far away from a place you loved? If so, how did the move affect you? What did you learn?

DIGGING DEEPER

See Isaiah 66:1–2a. Is God confined to particular places? Why do you think we sometimes feel closer to God in some places and not in others? How can we remedy this kind of thinking?

SOLACE IN THE MOUNTAINS

In the subsequent verses, we observe David vacillating between hope and discouragement.

20. Describe the word picture in Psalm 42:7. How does David express his misery?

DIGGING DEEPER

What do you think David means by the phrase "deep calls to deep"?

21. Have you ever felt that you were drowning in sorrow or frustration? Read Isaiah 43:1–3. Do these verses mean a Christian will never drown or die in a fire? What does God promise?

22. How might Isaiah 43:1–3 comfort you when you are discouraged? Can you apply these verses to a specific situation you are facing right now? If so, please share.

23. How does David express his hope in Psalm 42:8? How does he spend his days and nights? What attribute of God does he especially dwell on? (See also Psalm 13:5–6.)

Hope is a projection of the imagination; so is despair. Despair all too readily embraces the ills it foresees; hope is an energy and arouses the mind to explore every possibility to combat them. . . . In response to hope the imagination is aroused to picture every possible issue, to try every door, to fit together even the most heterogeneous pieces in the puzzle.
—Thornton Wilder,
Theophilus North

24. Do you tend to deny God's love for you when you are disheartened? Do you tend to believe that God should express his love to you by fixing all your problems? Why is this faulty thinking, based on lies?

25. How does David express his misery again in 42:9–10? How does he address God? What tension is evident?

26. What questions does he ask in verse 9? Are questions typical of the downhearted? Can they be helpful in the process of recovery? Why or why not?

27. In verse 10, David says his "bones suffer mortal agony." What are the physical effects of long-term sadness, even depression? If you or a loved one suffers with ongoing depression accompanied by physical symptoms, what action do you think should be taken?

THE KEY TO OVERCOMING SADNESS

28. As he concludes, the psalmist repeats verse 5. We also observe this refrain at the end of Psalm 43, a sister psalm of 42. This refrain contains the key to overcoming sadness and loss in life. What is the key? Rephrase this refrain in your own words.

> The psalmist felt, and publicly expressed, the gamut of emotions—from hurt to fury, from desire for vengeance to contempt against God. How comforting to know that we are not alone when we ache with loneliness, burn with anger, or tremble with fear. Someone before us has faced these emotions and, in the midst of that conflict, learned to love God.
> —Dan Allender and Tremper Longman
> (*Cry of the Soul*, 35–36)

29. Is there some sadness or loss in your life right now? If so, has this psalm helped you to heal and recover? Do you believe you will be joyful again? How might others in the group be a source of help? Please share.

Celebrate Each Day

Psalm 90

OPTIONAL

Memorize Psalm 90:14
Satisfy us in the morning with
your unfailing love, that we
may sing for joy and be glad
all our days.

Psalm 90 is the oldest psalm and is attributed to Moses. It may have been written during the wilderness wanderings when a generation of Israelites perished in the desert. Although we are not wandering in the desert, our days *are* numbered too. This reality should sober us, causing us to ask, how can my life be more productive? and, how can I make the most of the time God has given me?

Our service to God and others is another way to express our adoration. As you study this psalm, ask God to reveal ways you can honor him every moment of every day—especially in your work, as an act of worship.

 Read Psalm 90.

A SAFE PLACE

1. Moses paints a picture of God in 90:1. What is it? How does David express the same truth in Psalm 32:7?

2. How does Paul describe the same concept in New Testament terms (Romans 13:14; Galatians 3:27; Ephesians 6:10–11)?

3. What does it mean to you to "dwell" or "hide" in the Lord? To "clothe yourself" with Christ? Have you ever done this? If so, what differences did you experience?

4. How long has God protected those who come to him for refuge (Psalm 90:1)? How do you feel when you ponder this truth?

A CONTRAST IN TIME

5. In verse 2, Moses praises God for what attribute? How old is God?

6. In contrast, what is the fate of humankind (90:3)?

7. Why do all people experience this (see Genesis 3:17, 19; Romans 5:12)?

A watch in the night was about four hours.

A thousand years! How much may be crowded into it—the rise and fall of empires, the glory and obliteration of dynasties, countless events, all important to household and individual. Yet this period is to the Lord as nothing. In comparison with eternity, the most lengthened reaches of time are mere points; there is, in fact, no possible comparison between them.
—Charles Spurgeon
(*Psalms*, vol. 2, 21)

8. Psalm 90:4 explains that God and people perceive time differently. How is time different in God's economy than in ours? Why does this difference sometimes make life difficult for us?

9. From God's perspective, how long is a person's lifetime (90:5–6)?

10. Reflect on past years. Do your days seem to pass quickly or slowly? What have you learned regarding the passage of time?

11. How does the life of the young seem like new grass in the morning? How does the life of an elderly person seem like dry and withered grass? If you can identify with either of these images, share with your group any related insights.

Time is significant because it is so rare. It is completely irretrievable. You can never repeat it or relive it. There is no such thing as literal instant replay. That appears only on film. Time travels alongside us every day, yet it has eternity wrapped up in it. Although this is true, time often seems relative, doesn't it? For example, two weeks on a vacation is not at all like two weeks on a diet. Also, some people can stay longer in an hour than others can in a week! Ben Franklin said of time, "That is the stuff life is made of." Time forms life's building blocks. The philosopher William James once said, "The great use of life is to spend it for something that will outlast it."

—Lloyd Cory
(Swindoll, *Tale*, 571)

DIGGING DEEPER

Look up *eternity* or *eternal* in a Bible dictionary. What do you discover related to the character of God? What instances in Scripture show that God is Master over time?

12. Now Moses writes concerning the realities of living in a fallen world. What consequences must we all endure as a result? Why is God angry and indignant with humankind in general (90:7–9)?

13. Do you think God has the right to be angry with humankind? If so, why? If not, why not?

14. How is much of human life spent (90:10)? Has this been your experience?

15. How powerful is God's anger (90:11)?

DIGGING DEEPER

Read Exodus 15:3–10 and describe God's anger in the Song of Moses.

DIGGING DEEPER

Has the world ever experienced the full wrath of God? When will God's wrath be loosed on the earth? What will happen (Rev. 6:1–17; 14:14–20)?

16. When you see God in your mind's eye, do you see an angry God? If so, how might this perception influence your relationship with God and with others?

17. Psalm 90:11 states that God is to be "feared." Describe a healthy fear of God. In your opinion, what is an unhealthy fear?

18. Following the verses on God's wrath, Moses instructs us to "number our days" (90:12). Why do you think he includes this directive here?

19. What do you think it means to "number our days"? Approximately how many days have you lived? If you live to be seventy, how many more days on earth are yours? What lessons can you learn by working out these numbers?

Number Your Days (*5:22 minutes*). Are you at the mercy of whatever clamors for attention instead of focused on investing in what truly matters? Get some help with "establishing the work of your hands."

20. What will be the result of "numbering our days" (90:12)? Why do you think this happens?

DIGGING DEEPER

Locate and study a book on time management (for example, *The Time Trap* by Alec Mackenzie, now in its fourth edition). What principles can you glean to help you be more productive and efficient?

DIGGING DEEPER

Chart the way you spend your time for a day or a week. What do you learn? How do you waste time? What habits do you want to continue? Strategize a plan to become a better time manager so you can accomplish more in less time, giving you more opportunity to grow spiritually, serve God, rest, and celebrate life.

21. What can you do right now to "number your days"? Be specific. Share any related insight you have gleaned through the years as you have attempted to do this.

22. Instead of responding to humankind with anger, what does Moses ask God to do (90:13)?

> Here's the thing about God. He is so big and so perfect that we can't really understand Him. We can't possess Him, or apprehend Him. Moses learned this when he climbed up Mount Sinai and saw that the radiance of God's face would burn him up should he gaze upon it directly. But God so wants to be in relationship with us that He makes Himself small, smaller than He really is, smaller and more humble than His infinite, perfect self, so that we might be able to get to Him, a little bit.
> —Lauren Winner
> (*Girl Meets God*, 74)

23. Has God relented? What can you learn from Psalms 30:5 and 78:37–39?

DIGGING DEEPER

Wring out Romans 3:9–26
for a greater understanding
of why we should celebrate.

24. What happened to make God's compassion possible (Romans 5:8)?

25. In light of God's compassion, how does Moses suggest we respond, even when we experience trials and struggles (Psalm 90:14–15)? If you recall a time when you responded this way, please share.

26. In light of God's compassion, what does Moses request in verses 16–17a?

27. What is Moses' final request in 17b? What do you think he is asking?

Yesterday is a cashed check
and cannot be negotiated.
Tomorrow is a promis-
sory note and cannot be
utilized today. Today is cash
in hand. Spend it wisely.
—John Haggai
(*How to Win Over Worry*, 137)

28. What work would you like to see God "establish" in your life right now? What can you do to cooperate with him during the process?

"We do what we have
to do in order to do
what we want to do."
—James Farmer Jr. in
The Great Debaters (2007)

29. Look back over Psalm 90. What inspires you to be productive, celebrate life, and worship God?

Celebrate Security

Psalm 91

Twenty-four-hour news programming ensures that we are all aware of the latest threats—terrorism, child abductions, identity theft, dangerous chemicals in our food and air. Add these to fears that have plagued us for centuries like disease, war, and crime, and it's no wonder many people experience panic attacks and phobias. The world is a fallen, often dangerous place. Yet God reiterates throughout the Bible, "Fear not." Are you a fearful woman? You don't have to be. As you draw near to God, he promises to carry you through your fears to a safe and secure harbor. Psalm 91 is a beautiful expression of God's protection and ultimate deliverance. Understanding these wonderful realities gives you another reason to worship God with your whole heart.

 Read Psalm 91.

RESTING PLACES

1. What is the promise of verse 1?

OPTIONAL:

Memorize Psalm 91:1–2

Whoever dwells in the shelter of the Most High will rest in the shadow of the Almighty. I will say of the LORD, "He is my refuge and my fortress, my God, in whom I trust."

Both faith and fear sail into the harbor of your mind, but only faith should be allowed to anchor.
—Author unknown
(McKenzie, *14,000 Quips*, 174)

 Overcoming Fear (*2:40 minutes*). Wouldn't it be great to live without fear? God says that there is a kind of fear that will help us deal with all other fears.

Do a word study on Most
High God (*El Elyon*) and God
Almighty (*El Shaddai*). When
were they first used in the
Bible? What word pictures
can you discover related
to these names? How do
these pictures enrich your
understanding of God?

2. What two names does the author use to identify God in this verse? What do these names reveal about his character? How do these truths affect our ability to trust him?

3. Can you recall a time when you took shelter from an impending storm or disaster? Where did you go? How did you feel?

4. What do you think it means to "dwell" in "the shelter of the Most High"? What kind of "rest" might one find there?

5. Do you think this "rest" is guaranteed to every Christian or only those who "dwell" in that shelter? Do you dwell in God's presence or only run there occasionally when you are particularly frightened or worried?

The blessings here promised are not for all believers, but for those who live in close fellowship with God. Every child of God looks toward the inner sanctuary and the mercy-seat, yet all do not *dwell* in the most holy place; they run to it at times, and enjoy occasional approaches, but they do not habitually reside in the mysterious presence. Those who through rich grace obtain unusual and continuous communion with God, so as to abide in Christ and Christ in them, become possessors of rare and special benefits, which are missed by those who follow afar off, and grieve the Holy Spirit of God.
—Charles Spurgeon
(*Psalms*, vol. 2, 25)

In John 15, Jesus uses a metaphor to show us what it means to "dwell" or "abide" in God. Read verses 1–17. Who are the true vine and the gardener? What are the characteristics of one who dwells in that vine?

6. Has there been a particular time in your life when you were able to "rest" in God's shadow? Have you learned to live this way? If so, please share your experience with the group.

SECURE PLACES

Now the author elaborates by painting more word pictures to help us understand God's care for us.

7. What are the two word pictures in 91:2? Describe each. What is the psalmist telling us?

8. In verse 3, the psalmist says God will save us from the "fowler's snare." What is this? Use a dictionary if necessary. Who gets caught in it?

DIGGING DEEPER

During Bible times, where did communities find refuge from marauding bands of thieves or attacks from warring neighbors? What would the words, "He is my refuge and my fortress" have meant to the original audience? Consult a Bible dictionary or archaeological resource to learn more about this concept.

9. What are some modern day "fowler's snares"?

10. In 91:4, the author compares God to what creature? How is this creature protecting its offspring from the fowler's snare as well as other dangers?

11. Have you ever watched birds care for their young? If so, what did you observe and learn that might help us understand what the author wants to communicate through this comparison?

12. In 91:3, the psalmist also tells us that God will save us from "deadly pestilence." What is this? You may want to consult a dictionary. What might be the equivalent of "deadly pestilence" today?

13. Does this mean believers will never get sick or experience physical ailments? In your opinion, what does it mean?

14. Do you trust God with your physical health? What can you do to cooperate with him as he cares for you physically?

SECURE AT ALL TIMES

15. The writer refers to two more methods of defense that were common at that time (91:4). When would someone need a shield? What is a rampart? Use a dictionary if necessary. What is the author saying to his original audience and how do these truths apply to us today?

16. Because God is your faithful shield, you can overcome fears in your life. What fears are listed in verses 5–6?

17. Are you free from "the terror of night," even when you are alone? Specifically, what are you afraid of? If you have overcome this fear, share your insight.

If you have trouble sleeping, don't count sheep. Talk with the Shepherd.

18. Verse 5b refers to "the arrow that flies" at you. Who is shooting these arrows (see Ephesians 6:16)? What is his aim (1 Peter 5:8)?

19. What are some of the arrows he is shooting at you right now? Is your shield buffeting the arrows or are they reaching their mark? What can you do to protect yourself (Ephesians 6:10–11)? What do you think this means in practical terms?

SAFE FROM MY ENEMIES

DIGGING DEEPER

When will this ultimate punishment occur (Revelation 20:11–15; 21)? How will the world be different when all evil is destroyed?

20. The psalmist also promises that one day God's children will observe the ultimate punishment of the wicked (91:8). Do you look forward to this time? Why or why not?

21. What is the promise in 91:9–10? Again, what is the stipulation?

> Now faith is confidence
> in what we hope for
> and assurance about
> what we do not see.
> —Hebrews 11:1

22. How do you define *harm* or *disaster*? Does this mean you will never have trials or struggles? In your opinion, what does this mean?

23. Who has God enlisted in your protection (91:11)? What will they do (91:12)?

DIGGING DEEPER

Read Matthew 4:5–7, where Satan tempts Christ in the desert. Study the interchange. How does Satan foolishly apply Psalm 91:11–12? How does Jesus refute Satan? What are the lessons for us?

24. What will you be able to do as a result (91:13)? Who do you think is represented by "the great lion and the serpent" (1 Peter 5:8; Genesis 3:14)? What is the author teaching us?

SATISFACTION GUARANTEED

The psalm ends with God speaking about his beloved.

25. According to Psalm 91:14, what are two marvelous benefits of being under God's care?

The Psalms were sung by the Israelites in their homes during their daily routines, during celebrations, and also during worship times in the tabernacle, the temple, and later in the synagogues. How might you make the Psalms more a part of your daily life?   —Sue

26. In verse 15, the psalmist reveals other privileges. What are they?

27. What is the final benefit listed (91:16)? How long is your life going to last?

28. Are you a fearful person? If so, what frightens you most in life? Has the study of Psalm 91 helped you overcome your fears? Why or why not? The optional Scripture memorization for this lesson is Psalm 91:1–2. Consider memorizing that, or any other part of this psalm that might be particularly helpful. Can you think of creative ways you might help one another in the group to overcome your fears?

Celebrate Repentance

Psalms 51 and 32

What can hinder wholehearted worship of God Almighty? Our unconfessed sin can dampen our spirits, causing us to draw back from him. But the lesson of Psalms 51 and 32 is that the vilest of offenders can throw themselves on God's tender mercies and be restored to full fellowship.

 Read Psalm 51.

DEEP CLEANSING

1. What is David's plea in verses 1–2? On what two attributes of God's nature does he base his request?

OPTIONAL

Memorize Psalm 51:17
My sacrifice, O God, is a broken spirit; a broken and contrite heart you, God, will not despise.

The Hebrew word for sin in verse 2 is *chata*. It means to miss the mark—not measuring up to God's high standards, and none of us do. "For all have sinned and fall short of the glory of God" (Romans 3:23). That's why we all need a Savior.

 Repentance (*3:15 minutes*). Repentance is an important theological concept. What kind of repentance is required for salvation?

83

DIGGING DEEPER

Do a word study on the Hebrew term *hesed*, meaning *love*, found in verse 1. Where else do you find this term in the Bible? What do you learn about this amazing attribute of God?

Nathan risked his very life by confronting David. Without saying a word, David could have lifted his scepter, pointed it at Nathan, and the guards would have taken Nathan out and executed him.

2. (*For personal reflection*) Have you ever uttered a similar request? Do you believe you have committed a sin that is too grotesque for God to hear about? How do you picture God's countenance as you confess your wrongdoing?

 Read 2 Samuel 12:1–24.

In Psalm 51:3, David writes that he is keenly aware of his sin. Scan 2 Samuel 12:1–24 to discover the sinful events David now acknowledges. In the psalm, he has awakened to his sin, but for almost a year, he had rationalized and denied his sin.

3. In a nutshell, what was David's sin (2 Samuel 12:9)? How would you rate the seriousness of David's transgressions?

4. How did David respond to Nathan's confrontation (12:13a)? Nevertheless, what was the direct consequence of this sin (12:14)? What can we learn?

I have gotten to the point in my life where I am rarely surprised by my sin, just saddened by it. Surprise indicates that I did not think I was capable of such wrongdoing. I now know that is rarely the case. Sadness helps me understand my need for Jesus. Sadness at my thoughts, behaviors, actions—or lack thereof. Sadness helps me understand that without Him, I am lost.
—Nancy Ortberg
(*Looking for God*, 108)

5. Consider our culture. Do you think the values and mores of our society encourage us to deny our sins or recognize and deal with them? Can you give some examples?

6. What is your typical response when you realize you have sinned? How long does it normally take you to stop rationalizing and come to God with what you have thought, said, or done?

7. Later, after his confession, how did God comfort and bless David (12:24)? What can we learn?

THE ULTIMATE JUDGE

8. Who had David sinned against (Psalm 51:4a)?

9. Who is the ultimate Judge? What kind of judge is he (51:4)?

DIGGING DEEPER

David recognizes God's justice as an important part of his character. Why is this attribute important? Why can't God simply overlook our sin? What role does God's justice play in his plan of salvation?

 **Read Psalm 32.**

SEVERE MERCY

10. In Psalm 32:3–5, David expressed how he felt during the previous year of denial and rationalization. Read these verses and describe the effects of unconfessed sin.

11. Can you remember a time when you were "silent" concerning your sin? If so, how did you feel? Describe the experience and its effects.

12. What does David acknowledge about his nature in Psalm 51:5?

> There is no one on earth who is righteous, no one who does what is right and never sins.
> —Ecclesiastes 7:20

13. What do you believe is the essential nature of people? Are they born good or bad? Support your answer. (If you disagree with others in the group, please do so respectfully.)

> We must say of ourselves that we are evil, have been evil, and unhappily, I must add, shall be also in the future. Nobody can deliver himself; someone must stretch out a hand to lift him up.
> —Seneca, a pagan philosopher of Rome

DIGGING DEEPER

What doctrine is evident in verse 5? Refer to Romans 5:12–21, Job 14:1–4, and Genesis 8:20–21 to explain your understanding of this doctrine.

14. What does God most desire from David and from us (Psalm 51:6, 16–17)? Describe someone who personifies these words.

15. What do you think God means when he asks his people to develop "a broken and contrite heart"? What is the difference between "worm theology" and healthy humility?

16. Name specific ways you can develop "a broken and contrite heart."

A BLOOD BATH

17. How clean will David be when God cleanses him (Psalm 51:7; Isaiah 1:18)? What do you think he means?

Hyssop is a small bush with many woody twigs which made a natural sprinkler. It was used for scattering sacrificial blood in temple ceremonies on persons coming to be ritually cleansed.

DIGGING DEEPER

What do you think David means when he asks God to cleanse him with hyssop in verse 7?

18. In order to remain morally and emotionally strong after cleansing, David needs God's help. As a result, he makes several specific requests in the following verses. What are they and what do you think he means by each?

51:8a

51:8b

51:9

51:10

51:11

51:12

19. What is an appropriate response to a renewed relationship with God? What did David promise to do after God cleansed him (51:13–15)?

20. How have you expressed your gratitude to God for cleansing you of sin?

The kind of cry the psalmist describes can come either from the desperate (I *need* God and God alone) or the deliberate (I *want* God and God alone). Remember, we don't always have to wait until we're desperate. We can wise up enough to know how desperate we're going to be if we don't cry out immediately.
—Beth Moore
(*Get Out of That Pit*, 123)

21. To help us remain close to God, what does David advise us to do in Psalm 32:6a? Why (32:6b)?

Most scholars believe David continues to speak in Psalm 32:8–11.

22. What does David call God in 32:7? What will God do for him? Have you ever experienced this? If so, please share.

23. David had learned many lessons from this experience. What does he plan to do with what he has learned (32:8)? Are you willing to let others benefit from your experience? If so, how?

24. What is David's warning in verse 9? Does God need a "bit and bridle" to reign you in? Discuss the imagery and instruction in this verse.

25. In verses 10–11, David contrasts the lives of those who are right with God and those who are not. What awaits the wicked? The godly? How does one become "upright in heart" (see Romans 3:21–24)?

JOYFUL JUBILATION

The key word in the book of Psalms is *hallelujah*, that is, *praise the Lord*. This phrase has become a Christian cliché, but it is one that should cause a swelling of great emotion in the soul. Hallelujah, praise the Lord!
—J. Vernon McGee (*Psalms*, 7)

26. Joy accompanies a renewed and cleansed heart (Psalm 32:11). When you join with God's people to worship him, do you experience joy as you sing and praise him? If not, what do you need to do to enter into wholehearted worship and an unhindered relationship with your Creator?

27. In verse 2, David writes, "Blessed is the one whose sin the LORD does not count against them." Do you count sins against others? Against yourself?

28. What have you learned from David's experience as reflected in these two beautiful psalms?

Celebrate Forgiveness

Psalm 103

Psalm 103 is an Old Testament version of "Amazing Grace." This beautiful song calls us to worship God because of his incredible blessings, including forgiveness for our sin and shame. What is a fitting response? Charles Spurgeon has written:

> Many are our faculties, emotions, and capacities, but God has given them all to us, and they ought all to join in chorus to his praise. Half-hearted, ill-conceived, unintelligent praises are not such as we should render to our loving Lord. If the law of justice demanded all our heart and soul and mind for the Creator, much more may the law of gratitude put in a comprehensive claim for the homage of our whole being to the God of grace. (*Psalms*, vol. 2, 71)

May this "law of gratitude" draw us to worship God without restraint.

 Read Psalm 103.

AUTHENTIC WORSHIP

1. What is David modeling for us in verse 1? Name some ways you consistently bless or praise the Lord.

Some people are confused by the word "bless." God blesses us and we are told to bless God. "How can we be God's benefactor?" they rightly ask. The answer is to be found in the broader meaning of the Hebrew word which lies behind the translation. It is correctly rendered by the word "bless" but it means both to get good things from God and to give good things back to God. One of the few things we are in any position to return to God is praise; hence in this psalm and elsewhere "bless" means "praise."
—Robert Alden (*Psalms*, 11)

2. What does David remind us not to do (103:2)? Why are we prone to do this?

 Wounded (*3:46 minutes*). When a family member continuously wounds, the love of God makes forgiveness and healing possible.

A LIST OF DELIGHTS, JOYS, AND BENEFITS

3. David begins his list of benefits in verse 3 with *forgiveness*, a topic he treats more fully later in the psalm. We will tackle that topic later in the lesson. What is the second benefit?

4. Is David promising that Christians will never get sick? In what sense does God heal "all your diseases"?

5. Do you think there is any connection between our physical ailments and sin? Support your answer.

Unforgiveness is a poison we drink, hoping someone else will die.
—Author unknown

DIGGING DEEPER

Read and research James 5:13–16. How does your study inform David's statement in Psalm 103:3b, that God "heals all your diseases"?

6. What is the blessing in verse 4? Has this happened to you? If so, please share as you are comfortable.

A Turkish soldier had beaten a Christian prisoner until he was only half conscious, and while he kicked him he demanded, "What can your Christ do for you now?" The Christian quietly replied, "He can give me strength to forgive you."
—R. Earl Allen (Cory, *Quotable*, 143)

7. In verse 5, David reveals that God will satisfy our desires with good things. Is he promising a Rolls Royce, designer clothes, or a mansion? What does Jesus say in John 14:13?

In Psalm 103:5b, David says his "youth is renewed like the eagle's." What happens to an eagle each year that renews him? What do you think David is saying through this word picture?

8. Make a list of your desires. Which would bring glory to God? How can you rid yourself of unhealthy desires and replace them with desires that will result in God's glory as well as your joy?

9. In Psalm 103:6, David gives us another reason to praise God. What is it? In what sense do we enjoy this blessing now? In what sense will this ultimately be fulfilled in the future?

10. What is another wonderful privilege we enjoy today (103:7)? How does God make himself known to you?

11. Review the benefits described in verses 3–7. Which of these benefits have you experienced? Please elaborate on a specific incident.

THE BLESSING OF FORGIVENESS

12. Now David elaborates on the first blessing: forgiveness. He begins by reminding us of the character of God. What is God like (103:8–9)?

13. Specifically, what wonderful thing does God do for his children (103:10)? What do all people deserve from a holy God? What would we get if he repaid us "according to our iniquities" (see Romans 6:23)?

14. David paints two pictures to express the truth in Psalm 103:10. What are the two pictures in verses 11–12? What is he saying through this imagery?

15. Have you done something that you are afraid is beyond forgiveness? How do you feel as you read these verses? How much does God love you?

16. What is the mature response to past sin (Philippians 3:13–14)? How will your life be affected if you do not accept God's forgiveness?

17. Next David uses a domestic word picture to illustrate the truth of verse 10. Describe the word picture in Psalm 103:13. What is the author communicating?

18. David is assuming that fathers have compassion on their children. Is this always true? If you were raised by parents who lacked compassion, how did this affect your relationship with God? Can you share ways God is enabling you to overcome these hindrances?

Sin is removed from us by a miracle of love! If sin be removed so far, then we may be sure that the scent, the trace, the very memory of it must be entirely gone. There is no fear of its ever being brought back again. Our sins are gone; Jesus has borne them away. Glorify the Lord for this richest of blessings. The Lord alone could remove sin at all, and he has done it in a God-like fashion, making a final sweep of all our transgressions.
—Charles Spurgeon
(*Psalms*, vol. 2, 75–76)

19. What is one reason God forgives us (103:14)? Do you understand this reality about yourself and others? If so, how does this impact the way you see yourself and others? How about your expectations of yourself and others? How does this play out in your relationships?

20. How does David describe our lifetime on earth (103:15–16)?

21. In contrast, how long will believers live in the Lord's care (v. 17)?

22. In verse 17, David says that God's "righteousness" is with the children of believers. In what sense is this true? Is this a promise that the children of all believers will come to faith?

23. As a result of his everlasting love, what does God desire to see in his children (103:18)?

There is something God wants more than retribution. There is something He desires more than simply being paid back for the disrespect shown Him. God wants fellowship with us. And He was willing to put His own system of justice on hold while He made provision for sinful men and women to be rescued.
—Charles Stanley
(*Forgiveness*, 37)

DIGGING DEEPER

Jesus illustrated his power to forgive sins in Mark 2:1-12. Dissect the passage and explain what happened and how this supports the truth that God has the power to forgive sins.

24. In verse 19, David gives us a reason to believe that God is *able* to forgive us. What is it? Do you believe this verse is true? If so, will you accept the forgiveness he offers?

25. Because God is all powerful, who should praise him (103:20–21)?

26. What can you learn about "angels" and "heavenly hosts" from these verses?

27. What else should praise God (103:22a; Luke 19:37–40)?

28. Who else should celebrate the amazing wonders of our God (Psalm 103:22b)?

Once Abraham Lincoln was asked how he was going to treat the rebellious southerners when they had finally been defeated and had returned to the Union of the United States. The questioner expected that Lincoln would take a dire vengeance, but he answered, "I will treat them as if they had never been away."
—William Barclay,
*The New Daily Study Bible:
The Gospel of Luke*

29. David ends the psalm the same way he began. What is his response for all God has done for him (103:1a, 22b)? What is yours? What are some specific ways you can express your gratitude to God right now? This week? In the year ahead?

Celebrate the Cross

Psalm 22

Psalm 22 describes an execution much like a crucifixion, but David never experienced or even knew about this kind of execution. In fact, crucifixion was not invented by the Romans until centuries later. Therefore, most scholars interpret this psalm as a foreshadowing of Christ's agonizing death on the cross. David, as the author, may have been using poetic devices to express his own suffering, but these words became literally true when Jesus was crucified at the hands of his enemies. In a very real sense, Jesus is speaking through David. Psalm 22 is the psalm most quoted in the New Testament.

Why is this lesson titled "Celebrate the Cross"? Certainly, we would never celebrate anyone's suffering, and particularly not the suffering of the Son of God. However, what Jesus did on that cross gives all believers abundant reason to burst into song! And Psalm 22 gives us insight into the ordeal and meaning of the cross that we cannot find anywhere else.

 Read Psalm 22.

 Interpreting Psalm 22 (*3:19 minutes*).

OPTIONAL

Memorize Psalm 22:30–31

Posterity will serve him; future generations will be told about the Lord. They will proclaim his righteousness, declaring to a people yet unborn: He has done it!

God made him who had no sin to be sin for us, so that in him we might become the righteousness of God.
—2 Corinthians 5:21

1. Compare Psalm 22:1 and Matthew 27:45–46. Envision the setting of Jesus' crucifixion. Describe Jesus' emotional state at the moment he uttered those words.

DIGGING DEEPER

Investigate crucifixion, the Romans' hideous method of execution. What do you learn that will help the group understand what was actually happening to Jesus?

2. Assuming the words of Psalm 22 to be the words of Jesus, in verse 2, Jesus says he cries out by day and night. What has happened to make this possible (Matthew 27:45; Luke 23:44–45a)?

3. From Psalm 22:3–5, what do we learn about Jesus' inner feelings while he endured the cross?

4. Can you remember a time when you endured a particularly difficult experience? How did you feel? What part did your faith play?

He felt himself comparable to a helpless, powerless, downtrodden worm, passive while crushed, and unnoticed and despised by those who trod on him. He selects the weakest of creatures, which is all flesh; and becomes, when trodden upon, writhing, quivering flesh, utterly devoid of any might except to suffer.
—Charles Spurgeon
(*Psalms*, vol. 1, 80)

There were many who were appalled at him—his appearance was so disfigured beyond that of any human being and his form marred beyond human likeness.
—Isaiah 52:14

5. How did Jesus describe himself as he hung on the cross (Psalm 22:6a)? How did Isaiah describe him (see Isaiah 52:14 in sidebar)?

6. How is Jesus perceived and treated by those around him (Psalm 22:6b–7; Isaiah 53:3)? What details does Matthew reveal (Matthew 27:39–44)?

7. Compare the words of the mockers quoted in Psalm 22:8 with the words of the chief priests, teachers of the law, and the elders in Matthew 27:42–43. Do you think the Jewish leaders realized they were fulfilling a messianic prophecy with their words? Discuss.

8. Have you ever endured mocking or ridicule from others? How do you feel when you consider that Jesus can identify with you in this experience?

9. Now Jesus speaks concerning his humanity and his formative years. What had he learned as a youth that helped him now (Psalm 22:9–10)?

10. If you have been a Christian since you were a small child, share the benefits with the group.

BEASTS AND BRUTES

11. What is Jesus' plea in Psalm 22:11? Why is there no one to help him? Where are his disciples now (Matthew 26:56)?

12. Have you ever been abandoned by friends in time of need? If so, how did you feel? What did you learn?

13. Now Jesus describes the view from the cross. What three pictures does he paint in Psalm 22:12, 13, and 16a? Try to envision the scene. What do you think he is communicating with these words?

Bashan (Psalm 22:12) was a fertile region noted for its fine, well-fed cattle.

14. Have you or someone you know been threatened or hurt by wild animals? Discuss how it might feel to undergo such an experience.

THE AGONY OF CRUCIFIXION

DIGGING DEEPER

In the New Testament, what does Jesus reveal about himself and water (John 4:10, 13–14)?

15. In Psalm 22:14, Jesus says he is poured out like water. What do you think he means?

16. What does Jesus reveal about his bones (22:14)? His heart (22:14)? His hands and feet (22:16)?

17. In verse 15, Jesus says "My mouth is dried up like a potsherd." A potsherd is a piece of pottery. Do you know how pottery is processed? If so, can you shed any light on the meaning of Jesus' words?

18. Why do you think his tongue sticks to the roof of his mouth (22:15b)?
What is Jesus revealing about his suffering?

19. What can you learn about Jesus' physical condition and the experience
of crucifixion from verse 17?

20. In verse 18, we observe the fulfillment of another messianic prophecy. What is it? (See Matthew 27:35.)

A FINAL APPEAL

21. Summarize Jesus' final plea (Psalm 22:19–21). Pay close attention to the verbs. What emotions are evident? What is he asking?

God has rescued the Messiah who now expounds on the meaning of the cross.

22. Jesus' words in Psalm 22:22 are quoted in Hebrews 2:12. Read Hebrews 2:10–12. What can you learn about the relationship of Jesus and humankind? What is Jesus modeling for us in Psalm 22:22?

What happened that day when Y'Shua, God's Son, was on that cross can never fully be known. But a great deal of what happened that day is told to us in the Bible. The gospels describe the events of that day. The epistles explain the meaning of that day. The prophets foretell the importance of that day. But it is the psalms that let us know something of what Y'shua thought, how he suffered, what he prayed, the words of music that choked within the dryness of his throat. The most wonderful thing about the psalm of Passion if that it does not end in death . . . Y'shua sings another day!
—Ronald Allen
(*Lord of Song*, 118)

23. What did God the Father do for Christ (Psalm 22:24)? Has he ever done the same for you or anyone you know? If so, please share.

24. Now the Messiah prophesies, showing us what he accomplished on the cross (22:26–31). List the ways the world is different because Jesus was willing to go to the cross. What does the future hold? How do you feel as you read these verses?

25. The last phrase of the psalm, "He has done it," can also be translated as Jesus' last words on the cross. What were his last words (John 19:30)? What has Jesus done (Romans 3:21–26)?

But he was pierced for our transgressions, he was crushed for our iniquities; the punishment that brought us peace was on him, and by his wounds we are healed.
—Isaiah 53:5

26. How would your life be different if Jesus had not endured the cross?

When you were dead in your sins and in the uncircumcision of your flesh, God made you alive with Christ. He forgave us all our sins, having canceled the charge of our legal indebtedness, which stood against us and condemned us; he has taken it away, nailing it to the cross.
—Colossians 2:13–14

27. What is your reasonable response to what Jesus accomplished on the cross? How do you plan to thank him? Be specific.

There's nothing small or inconsequential about our stories. There is, in fact, nothing bigger. And when we tell the truth about our lives— the broken parts, the secret parts, the beautiful parts— then the gospel comes to life, an actual story about redemption, instead of abstraction and theory and things you learn in Sunday school.
—Shauna Niequist
(*Bittersweet*, 240)

Celebrate the Crown

Psalm 98

Last week, in our study of Psalm 22, we beheld the suffering Messiah on the cross. In contrast, in this lesson we see the *King of kings and Lord of lords* returning to rule and reign. Psalms 96 through 99 are called royal psalms because they reveal his return to make all things right, bright, and beautiful. What is the proper response to this marvelous news? Only boundless worship and adoration!

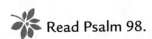 **Read Psalm 98.**

SING A NEW SONG!

1. The psalm opens with the mandate, "Sing to the LORD a new song." Why will we do this (98:1)?

Worship Together (*3:01 minutes*). It's going to happen in eternity, so we might as well start now!

OPTIONAL

Memorize Psalm 98:1–2

Sing to the LORD a new song, for he has done marvelous things; his right hand and his holy arm have worked salvation for him. The LORD has made his salvation known and revealed his righteousness to the nations.

Music lives as music progresses. We are heirs to the treasures of the ages. It all belongs to us because it all belongs to him. All the best music of the ages and cultures of man may be used to praise the Lord of Song. Music is his. He gives it to us as his gift. We return it to him with joy in worship.
—Ronald Allen
(*Lord of Song*, 149)

The call for a new song is not just a desire to throw out the old hymnals. The best of the old songs will always be new when they are sung with understanding.
—Ronald Allen
(*Lord of Song*, 152–53)

2. What is the verb tense of the second part of verse 1? What does this verb tense tell you?

3. Revelation 21:1–4 reveals details concerning this glorious time. Read the passage. What do you learn about this new era?

4. According to Psalm 98:2–3, who will know about God's salvation, offered to humankind through Christ? How do you think those who have rejected Christ will feel?

5. Who do you know right now that needs to know Christ? Consider ways to befriend this person so that you might one day introduce him or her to Jesus. Discuss.

DIGGING DEEPER

Read *Questioning Evangelism* by Randy Newman. What concepts are presented that challenge and inspire you?

Who will enter to worship?
Those who worship God
before they have approached
the church building. And
when they enter the building, they enter deliberately
to do in public that which
they have already done in
private: to adore the living
God. Further, they come
to worship together!
—Ron Allen and
Gordon Borror
(*Worship*, 51)

6. Who will go into God's kingdom together during this new era (Revelation 7:9)? In light of this truth, how do you think God wants you to treat people of different ethnic backgrounds and races? What will you say to your brothers and sisters in the kingdom if you have not been their "neighbor" now (James 2:8–9)?

7. In Psalm 98:3, what particular ethnic group is singled out as God's beloved? How do you feel as you consider this truth?

8. How can Christians and the church be more intentional about loving people of different races and ethnic backgrounds?

9. Do you struggle to include people you don't understand? How might you prepare for a multiethnic future with God and all his people?

10. Who will praise the Lord when he brings in his kingdom? What is a way to praise him (98:4)?

11. Do you like to sing? What part has singing and vocal music played in your life? Why do you think God created us with the capacity to sing?

12. What is another way to praise the King (vv. 5–6)?

13. Do you now or have you ever played a musical instrument? If so, do you praise God with it? Expound on the experience.

> God's praises should be performed in the best possible manner, but their sweetness mainly lies in spiritual qualities. The concords of faith and repentance, the harmonies of obedience and love are true music in the ear of the Most High.
> —Charles Spurgeon
> (*Psalms*, vol. 2, 54)

14. Do you have personal preferences related to music and instruments used in congregational worship? What do you especially enjoy about this particular kind of music?

15. What kinds of music do you think will characterize worship in the new era full of people from a variety of ethnic backgrounds who have lived over many centuries?

16. Do you insist that others honor your musical preferences? Are you willing to honor theirs? Discuss this issue and the conflict it has caused for many believers today. What solutions can you suggest?

17. When the Lord brings in his kingdom, what will be the effect on nature (98:7–8)?

18. Why do you think the earth is rejoicing? What is nullified when the Lord brings in his ultimate kingdom (Genesis 3:17–19)? How will life change as a result?

We have [a] new song because he has come, and seen and conquered. Jesus, our King, has lived a marvelous life, died a marvelous death, risen by a marvelous resurrection, and ascended marvelously into heaven. By his divine power he has sent forth the Holy Spirit doing marvels, and by that sacred energy his disciples have also wrought marvelous things and astonished all the earth. Idols have fallen, superstitions have withered, systems of error have fled, and empires of cruelty have perished. For all this he deserves the highest praise.
—Charles Spurgeon
(*Psalms*, vol. 2, 52–53)

19. According to Psalm 98:9, what is another reason the whole earth will rejoice when Christ returns to rule and reign? (See also Psalm 96:10–13.)

20. Do you need to fear God's judgment? If you are God's child, what is the promise of Romans 8:1? What do you think this means?

21. The following passages reveal the nature of judgment for believers. This judgment is called the *Bema* seat and does not affect where believers will spend eternity. Read the Scriptures carefully. What do you discover?

1 Corinthians 3:10–15

Revelation 4:1–4, 10–11

DIGGING DEEPER

Research the origin of the name *Bema*. Why is it an appropriate name for the believer's judgment?

DIGGING DEEPER

Revelation 20:11–14 reveals the nature of the judgment for those who reject Christ. This is called the great white throne judgment. What can you learn from this passage? What differences do you observe between this judgment and the *Bema* judgment for believers?

LET JUSTICE ROLL DOWN

22. Read Psalm 99:4. What does the King love? What kind of world will he establish?

Away with the noise of your songs! I will not listen to the music of your harps.
But let justice roll on like a river, righteousness like a never-failing stream!
—Amos 5:23–24

23. Do you long for a world of justice and equity? Specifically, what would that world look like? What can you do right now to make this world more just and equitable?

LOOKING BACK, LOOKING FORWARD

Look backward—see
    Christ dying for you.
Look upward —see Christ
    pleading for you.
Look inward—see Christ
    living in you.
Look forward—see Christ
    coming for you.
        —Author unknown
        (Cory, *Quotable*, 61)

24. As you contemplate your eternal future where the Lord rules and reigns, how do you feel? How will your life be different once Christ returns and takes over?

25. How does this knowledge affect the way you live and worship today? Please share.

26. Review the lessons in this guide. What roadblocks to authentic worship have you overcome?

27. What have you learned that will enrich your worship of Almighty God through your lifetime?

My favorite places on earth are on the beach, in the mountains, and in the church. On the shore, I love to watch the waves roll in as they seem to speak the name of my Fairest Lord Jesus. And on a mountaintop where the wind and trees ring out his majestic name. And in the midst of my sweet church community singing together his praises and glory. God created us to praise, and what a privilege and wonder it is! —Sue

It's rebellious, in a way, to choose joy, to choose to dance, to choose to love your life. It's much easier and much more common to be miserable.
　　　—Shauna Niequist
　　　(*Cold Tangerines*, 234)

28. Encourage the women in your group. Who has made you feel wel-
come? Who has ministered to you? Who have you appreciated and
why? Who have you seen grow closer to the Lord and deeper in their
worship? Be sure to tell these people what they have meant to you
during the study.

29. What's next? How do you plan to keep growing closer to Christ?

Works Cited

Alden, Robert. *Psalms*. Vol. 3, *Songs of Discipleship*. Chicago: Moody Press, 1976.

Allen, Ronald. *Lord of Song*. Portland, OR: Multnomah, 1985.

Allen, Ronald, and Gordon Borror. *Worship: Rediscovering the Missing Jewel*. Portland, OR: Multnomah, 1982.

Allender, Dan, and Tremper Longman. *Cry of the Soul*. Colorado Springs, CO: NavPress Publishing Group, 1994.

Barger, Lilian Calles. *Chasing Sophia: Reclaiming the Lost Wisdom of Jesus*. San Francisco, CA: Josey-Bass, 2007.

Barton, Ruth Haley. *Sacred Rhythms: Arranging Our Lives for Spiritual Transformation*. Downers Grove, IL: InterVarsity, 2006.

Cory, Lloyd, comp. *Quotable Quotations*. Wheaton, IL: Victor Books, 1985.

DeClaisse-Walford, Nancy L. *Introduction to the Psalms: A Song from Ancient Israel*. St. Louis, MO: Chalice Press, 2004.

Haggai, John Edmund. *How to Win Over Worry*. Updated edition. Eugene, OR: Harvest House, 2001.

Jensen, Irving. *Psalms: A Self-Study Guide*. Chicago: Moody Press, 1968.

Lamott, Anne. *Grace (Eventually): Thoughts on Faith*. New York: Riverhead Books, 2007.

McGee, J. Vernon. *Psalms, chap. 42–89*. Thru-the-Bible Commentary Series. Nashville: Thomas Nelson, 1991.

McKenzie, E. C., comp. *14,000 Quips & Quotes: For Speakers, Writers, Editors, Preachers, and Teachers*. Grand Rapids: Baker, 1990.

Moore, Beth. *Get Out of That Pit: Straight Talk About God's Deliverance*. Nashville: Integrity, 2007.

Niequist, Shauna. *Bittersweet: Thoughts on Change, Grace, and Learning the Hard Way*. Grand Rapids: Zondervan, 2010.

Niequist, Shauna. *Cold Tangerines*. Grand Rapids: Zondervan, 2007.

Ortberg, Nancy. *Looking for God*. Carol Stream, IL: Tyndale, 2008.

Spurgeon, Charles. *Psalms*. 2 volumes. The Crossway Classic Commentaries, ed. Alister McGrath and J. I. Packer. Wheaton, IL: Crossway, 1993.

Stanley, Charles. *Forgiveness*. Nashville: Thomas Nelson, 1987.

Swindoll, Charles R. *Hope Again*. Dallas: Word Publishing, 1996.

Swindoll, Charles R. *Living Beyond the Daily Grind*. New York: Inspirational Press, 1988.

Ten Boom, Corrie. *Clippings from My Notebook*. Nashville, TN: Thomas Nelson, 1982.

Tozer, A.W. *Worship: The Missing Jewel of the Evangelical Church*. Harrisburg, PA: Christian Publications, Inc., 1961.

Walvoord, John, and Roy Zuck. *The Bible Knowledge Commentary: Old Testament*. Wheaton, IL: Victor Books, 1985.

Winner, Lauren F. *Girl Meets God: A Memoir*. New York: Random House, 2007.

About the Author

Sue Edwards is associate professor of Christian education (her specialization is women's studies) at Dallas Theological Seminary where she has the opportunity to equip men and women for future ministry. She brings over thirty years of experience into the classroom as a Bible teacher, curriculum writer, and overseer of several megachurch women's ministries. As minister to women at Irving Bible Church and director of women's ministry at Prestonwood Baptist Church in Dallas, she has worked with women from all walks of life, ages, and stages. Her passion is to see modern and postmodern women connect, learn from one another, and bond around God's Word. Her Bible studies have ushered thousands of women all over the country and overseas into deeper Scripture study and community experiences.

With Kelley Mathews, Sue has coauthored *New Doors in Ministry to Women: A Fresh Model for Transforming Your Church, Campus, or Mission Field*; *Women's Retreats: A Creative Planning Guide*; and *Leading Women Who Wound: Strategies for an Effective Ministry*. Sue and Kelley joined with Henry Rogers to coauthor *Mixed Ministry: Working Together as Brothers and Sisters in an Oversexed Society*.

Sue has a doctor of ministry degree from Gordon-Conwell Theological Seminary in Boston and a master's in Bible from Dallas Theological Seminary. With Dr. Joye Baker, she oversees the Dallas Theological Seminary doctor of ministry degree in Christian education with a women-in-ministry emphasis.

Sue has been married to David for forty years. They have two married daughters, Heather and Rachel, and five grandchildren. David is a CAD applications engineer, a lay prison chaplain, and founder of their church's prison ministry.